MW01060846

God Loves You
Just the Way
You Are

Blue Mountain Arts®

New and Best-Selling Titles

By Susan Polis Schutz:
To My Daughter with Love on the Important Things in Life
To My Son with Love

By Douglas Pagels:
For You, My Soul Mate
Required Reading for All Teenagers
The Next Chapter of Your Life
You Are One Amazing Lady

By Marci:
Friends Are Forever
10 Simple Things to Remember
To My Daughter
To My Mother
To My Sister
You Are My "Once in a Lifetime"

By Wally Amos, with Stu Glauberman:
The Path to Success Is Paved with Positive Thinking

By M. Butler and D. Mastromarino:
Take Time for You

By James Downton, Jr.:
Today, I Will... Words to Inspire Positive Life Changes

By Carol Wiseman:
Emerging from the Heartache of Loss

Anthologies:
A Daughter Is Life's Greatest Gift
A Son Is Life's Greatest Gift
Dream Big, Stay Positive, and Believe in Yourself
God Is Always Watching Over You
Hang In There
The Love Between a Mother and Daughter Is Forever
The Peace Within You
There Is Nothing Sweeter in Life Than a Granddaughter
Think Positive Thoughts Every Day
When I Say I Love You
Words Every Woman Should Remember

God Loves You Just the Way You Are

...and He Will Always Be There for You

Edited by Becky McKay

Blue Mountain Press™
Boulder, Colorado

Copyright © 2014 by Blue Mountain Arts, Inc.

Scripture quotations are from *The Holy Bible, New International Version*®, NIV®. Copyright © 1973, 1978, 1984, 2011 by Biblica, Inc.® Used by permission. All rights reserved worldwide.

Library of Congress Control Number: 2013951094
ISBN: 978-1-59842-793-6

Acknowledgments appear on page 92.

Printed in China.
First Printing: 2014

⊕ This book is printed on recycled paper.

This book is printed on paper that has been specially produced to be acid free (neutral pH) and contains no groundwood or unbleached pulp. It conforms with the requirements of the American National Standards Institute, Inc., so as to ensure that this book will last and be enjoyed by future generations.

Blue Mountain Arts, Inc.
P.O. Box 4549, Boulder, Colorado 80306

Contents
(Authors listed in order of first appearance)

Lisa Mae Huddleston

Amanda Rowe

Barbara Cage

Rachel Snyder

Linda E. Knight

Barbara J. Hall

Selina Maybury

Dzana Madagu

Jeff Seaman

Sydney Nealson

Mark Batterson

Donna Fargo

Jason Blume

Jenna Lucado Bishop

Alin Austin

Nancye Sims

Caroline J. Hewitt

Perri Elizabeth Hogan

Candy Paull

Debbie Burton-Peddle

Lamisha Serf

Cathleen Zeller

Ashley Rice

Douglas Pagels

John Ortberg

Paul David Tripp

Janice Pettit

Ernest Holmes

Charles R. Swindoll

Desmond Tutu

Lisa J. Butler

Susan Hickman Sater

Dr. David Jeremiah

Suzy Toronto

Joanne Simon

Stormie Omartian

Holley Gerth

Paula Finn

God Loves You
Just the Way You Are

You are loved by God.
He chose you
before you were born.
He speaks to your heart every day.
His desire is for you to know
how much He loves you.
There is no need to worry
or be anxious about anything.
Everything you have experienced in life
had a purpose —
to bring you to where you are today.
In knowing this,
may your heart be light.
May you know without a doubt
that God loves you and chose you
just the way you are.

— Lisa Mae Huddleston

Trust in God's Dream for Your Life

God has a dream for your life.
Everything, past and present,
is God's way of preparing you
for your destiny.
God's dreams for you are so big.
He uses every event in your life
to fulfill His purpose for you.
His love for you cannot be measured.
It is completely flawless,
absolutely faithful, and totally amazing.

Remember all that God has done.
Hold on to it.
Cherish each moment in your heart.
Remember that you are not alone;
His arms are always open.
Rest in His presence and have confidence
in the place to which He is leading you.

When walking in this truth,
amazing things can happen
if you simply believe.
His love and thoughts toward you
are endless.
You can change the world by saying yes
to the promise that is already yours.
It is your time to step out.
Love your life… it's a gift from God
that He will continually use
to spread His goodness through you.

Be blessed.
God will never stop blessing you.
He will never stop loving you.
In His eyes, you are amazing.

— Lisa Mae Huddleston

The Meaning of Faith

Faith does not mean
that everything will work out
exactly as you hoped,
but that when it doesn't,
you will not become bitter.

Faith does not mean
that you will not experience heartbreak,
but that when you do, you will heal.

Faith does not mean
that you will never make mistakes,
but that when you do,
you will try your best to set them right.

Faith does not mean
that you will never be lonely,
but that when you are,
you will know that you are not truly alone.

Faith does not mean
that you will never lose,
but that you will never lose hope.

— Amanda Rowe

Faith Is...

☆ Facing life's challenges and trials with hope, dignity, patience, and peace.

☆ Anticipating the best in life and in others.

☆ Imagining that anything is possible and that dreams do come true.

☆ Trusting in yourself, your loved ones, and God.

☆ Hoping that what can go right will and that love, joy, and peace will always prevail.

— Barbara Cage

When all else fades and melts away, faith remains. Like a flower that blossoms in the midst of a storm, your faith will grow and bloom when you least expect it.

When you feel you've prayed every prayer and wished every wish, faith will knock gently and ask to be let in. Choose faith and you choose life. Choose faith and you choose courage. Choose faith and you choose to follow the urgings of your spirit, no matter what hardships are tearing at your heart.

There is no test to prove yourself worthy of faith. Simply invite her in, and you'll feel the arms of faith wrap around you and embrace you with quiet comfort. You'll rest in the knowing that faith is an unspoken prayer that will never leave your side.

— Rachel Snyder

God Will Take Care of You

May your heart
find peace and comfort in the knowledge
that you are never alone.
May God's presence give you rest.
He knows how you feel.
He is ever aware of your circumstances
and ready to be your strength,
your grace, and your peace.

He is there to cast sunlight
into all your darkened shadows,
to send encouragement through the love
of friends and family,
and to replace your weariness
with new hope.
God is your stronghold,
and with Him as your guide,
you need never be afraid.
No circumstances can block His love.
No grief is too hard for Him to bear.
No task is too difficult
for Him to complete.
When what you are feeling
is simply too deep for words
and nothing anyone does or says
can provide you with the relief you need,
God understands.

— Linda E. Knight

How Much Does God Love You?

Do you ever look up to see the stars at night?
Have you tried to count them all
or imagine their number,
feeling small and insignificant
and overwhelmed at the sight?

Do you ever try to picture
the hand that put each star in its place,
that knows their number,
and — more importantly —
knows that you are looking up
to see the vastness of His universe?
He sees your face, hears your thoughts,
and reads your heart.

God loves you more than
    all the stars in heaven.
There's an endless amount of love
    that He is always sending you,
and His love is there to cover
    every moment of your life.

— Barbara J. Hall

For I am convinced that neither death
nor life, neither angels nor demons,
neither the present nor the future, nor
any powers, neither height nor depth,
nor anything else in all creation, will be
able to separate us from the love of God.

— Romans 8:38-39 (NIV)

Always remember
that God is not like us.
He is wondrous, amazing,
and beyond our capability
to comprehend.

God is not judgmental —
He understands the motivations
behind your choices and actions,
and His compassion is boundless.
God knows every inch of your being.
He loves all the good things about you,
and He freely forgives you
for your flaws and mistakes.

God knows intimately that you are
like no other person on earth,
and He loves you uniquely.

God is light and life and joy.
He is evident in every smile
that crosses your face.
God is always with you —
supporting you, blessing you,
teaching you, and above all loving you
with a love beyond human understanding.

— Selina Maybury

Believe in How Special You Are

Even though you may not fully realize it,
you were created with all it takes
to achieve in this life.
It may seem like others are getting ahead
while you are still figuring out
who you are.
Please do not despair
or become discouraged.
Take a look in the mirror
at the many wonderful things about you.
Have you ever seen anyone
who smiles like you?
Things you think aren't important
are the very tools that bless you.
Believe in how special you are
and appreciate yourself...
even if others don't.
Tell yourself that you are a priceless gift —
an invaluable and amazing person
created to make a big difference.

— Dzana Madagu

When God made you He broke the mold... If you were to search the whole world, you wouldn't find two people who had the same footprint or fingerprint or voiceprint. You are unique. Why did God make you different from every person who's ever lived? Why did He go to all that trouble? Because He wants you to know how special you are, how much you matter to Him.

— Jeff Seaman

You should feel really good... about who you are. About all the great things you do! Appreciate your uniqueness. Acknowledge your talents and abilities. Realize what a beautiful soul you have. Understand the wonder within.

— Sydney Nealson

☆ God believes in you.

☆ He's given you unique gifts and talents,
and He wants you to make the most of them.

☆ He knows you can do anything you set
your mind to.

☆ He rejoices in every goal you reach and
every dream you turn into reality.

There has never been and never will be anyone else like you. But that isn't a testament to you. It's a testament to the God who created you. You are unlike anyone who has ever lived. But that uniqueness isn't a virtue. It's a responsibility. Uniqueness is God's gift to you, and uniqueness is your gift to God. You owe it to yourself to *be yourself.* But more important, you owe it to the One who designed you and destined you.

— Mark Batterson

God Gifted You to Do Something Special

Accept yourself — faults and all — and don't ever let what you perceive as negative traits weigh you down. Change them if you need to and make them work for you instead of against you.

Respect your body, mind, and spirit. Guard your health. Don't become addicted to anything. Fill your mind with positive thoughts. Think of the consequences of your actions before you act. Let your conscience be your guide. Don't do anything you'd be ashamed to tell the truth about, and always be honest with yourself.

Don't try to change others; love them, even if you don't love their actions. Don't allow yourself to feel superior or inferior to people because of their position in life, their vocation, their appearance or fortune, or the value the world places on them. Live your life in a spirit of cooperation with others; good relationships are built on "win-win" situations.

Always act for the highest and noblest good. Trust that there's a divine plan for your life. Do your best. Be passionate about everything you do, but don't become so attached to the outcome. Don't worry about some mistake you've made. Once it's done, it's over and out of your hands. Learn the lesson, ask for forgiveness if you need to, and move on.

Remember that each of us is gifted to do something special for the universe. Celebrate your gift and give it to others with love, and more joy and love and inspiration will come to you.

— Donna Fargo

You Are God's Masterpiece

He doesn't make mistakes,
and He had a plan
when He made you
the beautiful person
that you are.

You may not always believe it,
but you are truly unique
and very important.

It's easy to compare ourselves
to those around us
and to feel as though
we're not good enough.

But God loves all His children,
and each one is in this world for a reason.
Let yourself bask in the warmth of His love,
knowing that He created you
and accepts you as you are.

— Jason Blume

When God sees you, He cannot help but smile and sigh with satisfaction. *What a masterpiece!* He must think. *I made no mistake when I breathed her into existence or when I knit him together.* He sees a work of art more valuable than any Leonardo da Vinci at the Louvre.

— Jenna Lucado Bishop

God Sends Blessings in the Form Of...

☆ The potential of a brand-new day.

☆ An unexpected gift.

☆ A supportive, loving family.

☆ Health and wellness.

☆ A phone call from a good friend.

☆ Your favorite song on the radio.

☆ Fresh mountain air.

☆ A hearty laugh.

☆ A delicious meal.

☆ All the little things that are sometimes taken for granted.

May God Grant You These Gifts

Beautiful days filled with good health and all the happiness you deserve.

Appreciation of the beauty that surrounds you in His wonder-filled world.

The love and the knowledge that you are — and will always be — His cherished child.

Hope even when it's hard to imagine that the sun will shine again.

Strength when the road becomes hard and you feel too weary to take one more step.

The faith and peace that come from knowing He will always be there for you.

The knowledge that you have all you need to overcome any obstacle in your way.

— Jason Blume

A Comforting Reminder

If you need to lean on someone,
   there is no greater strength.
If you need to move away from
   difficulty and toward resolve,
   there is no greater direction to go in.
If you wish to walk with happiness,
   there is no greater
   traveling companion…

God will be there for you.

If you are filled with questions,
   there is no better place to look
   for the answers.
If you are troubled, there is no
   refuge more safe and secure.
If you wish to reach for a star,
   there are no words of encouragement
   greater than His are.
If you seek serenity, understanding,
   and joy, then follow your heart
   when it tells you to believe.

For God will be there for you.

— Alin Austin

God Is Everywhere…

☆ In the eyes of someone you love.

☆ In a star-filled sky.

☆ In a kitten's purr.

☆ In the soft skin of a newborn.

☆ In the calm before the storm and in the rainbow after.

He is the light of this day.
He is the sky above you,
the earth beneath you,
and the life of every living thing.

He is in every smile,
in every thought that gives you hope,
in every tear that waters your soul,
and in every moment you can't
face alone.

He's in the friends you meet along the way —
in strangers you have yet to meet
and blessings you have yet to receive.

He's in every good thing
that touches you.

— Nancye Sims

Reach out to God, and He Will Give You Strength

He gives strength to the weary and increases the power of the weak. Even youths grow tired and weary, and young men stumble and fall; but those who hope in the Lord will renew their strength. They will soar on wings like eagles; they will run and not grow weary, they will walk and not be faint.

— Isaiah 40:29-31(NIV)

True strength is measured
by your inner resolve
to stand tall with pride intact.
True strength reveals itself
as you stand firm to your beliefs.
True strength dares
to say no to temptations
that may lead you off course,
for you have your life to live
and you choose to live it
by honoring who and what
you are meant to become.

You can endure anything
if it means staying true to yourself,
for you have a gift called true strength.

— Caroline J. Hewitt

Hold on to Your Faith

Life just doesn't seem fair sometimes.
Bad things happen to the best people,
and there are no explanations
to help us understand why.

These are the moments
when faith helps you recover
and prayer comes into play.
Let your faith carry you
through your strife.
Let it bolster your heart
and ease your pain.

Let your faith remind you
that you are loved
and that God doesn't give burdens
that are impossible to bear.
Remember how many of your prayers
have been answered,
even when you didn't expect them to be.
Life has a way of leveling out
beyond these trials.

Hold on to your faith.
Hold on to His love.
The good will come back to you...
because you believe.

— Perri Elizabeth Hogan

Angels Are Watching over You

There are angels among us.
You may have encountered
    one lately.
It may have been someone
who offered an encouraging word,
    a helping hand,
        or a simple smile.
Angels know how to touch
    through human hands
        and love through human hearts.
It doesn't take a miracle to recognize
    when an angel has been at work.

Just open your eyes
   and watch for love in action.
Angels are everywhere.
Seen or unseen, they lift spirits,
   encourage the downhearted,
      and offer heavenly help
         for down-to-earth problems.

If you hear the sound of wings, remember:
   angels are watching over you.

— Candy Paull

God Doesn't Expect Perfection

No one is perfect. We all make mistakes; there are no predictors of the outcomes of our decisions. However, mistakes do help us learn and grow, offering us methods for improvement.

Don't be too hard on yourself. Think of all you've accomplished and the good things you have going for you. Think of how positively you've affected others in your life.

Trust your instincts and continue to live with your integrity and values. With each passing day, you'll feel more and more confident in how you're doing. Know that everything will be just fine.

— Debbie Burton-Peddle

God Loves You Even When…

☆ You don't love yourself.

☆ You make mistakes.

☆ You take His blessings for granted.

☆ You are in a bad mood.

☆ You think you don't deserve His love.

We Are All Works in Progress

Sometimes in life we are disappointed in ourselves for one reason or another. Maybe we expect more from ourselves than we do from others, or maybe we simply wish we had done things differently. We all experience this from time to time, and the only thing we can do is know that we can and will move on.

Tomorrow will come and we will have yet another opportunity for growth. We can put today behind us and work to do better and be better than we were yesterday.

Change takes time, and so we must be patient with others and ourselves. We must understand that growth is a process and that transformation doesn't happen instantly.

Whatever it is you wish you hadn't done or had done differently, let it go. You have another opportunity tomorrow to make it different. It just takes time, so be patient with yourself and cut yourself some slack.

We are all works in progress.

— Lamisha Serf

A Prayer for Help

Let me remember, Lord,
to be myself —
and to be glad for this opportunity
to be me.
Help me, Lord, to remember
that my opinions are right
for my life only,
and they don't extend
into other people's lives
unless they are invited in.
Help me be careful
not to offer more
than someone else wants to hear.
I want to curtail that urge to rearrange
someone else's life
or to correct mistakes
that aren't my own.

Remind me that I can't change
anyone but me...
and I'm not supposed to.
As I go through this day, Lord,
give me the strength and wisdom
to be me.
Give me the gift of listening and caring.
Remind me that without you
I can't even take care of myself...
and give me the peace in knowing
you will take care of everyone else too.

— Barbara J. Hall

Wouldn't every day be wonderful if you could see yourself the same way God does — as a beautiful creation created for a specific purpose and plan? As someone who is valued, cherished, seen as a wonderful treasure, and given a love so unconditional and perfect you can't even comprehend it?

You were designed by the hand of God. You may sometimes make mistakes or fall short of your expectations, dreams, and desires — but don't we all? Failures are just one of life's little experiences. They're a tool to grow with and learn from. They aren't given to stop you from moving forward, but rather to inspire you to be strengthened, look ahead with determination, and go on with endurance.

If you learn to love and accept yourself, it becomes much easier to love others and be tolerant of their faults. Your life can be more joyful if you see the good instead of the bad and realize just how beautiful this world is.

Look at yourself with a heart full of love, understanding, forgiveness, kindness, and gentleness. Remember that you matter enough to have been created by a God who crafted you in His image and designed you to fulfill a purpose that fits into His plans. You are important to God.

— Cathleen Zeller

There's a Light
Inside You

There's a light inside you
that is brighter than sunshine.
There's a hope inside you
that can get you through anything.
There's a strength inside you
that is so great that
whatever comes your way today,
you can face it —
with heart, courage, and love.

— Ashley Rice

You are something — and someone —
very special. You really are. There are so
many beautiful things about you. You're
a one-of-a-kind treasure, uniquely here
in this space and time. You are here
to shine in your own wonderful way,
sharing your smile in the best way you
can, and remembering all the while that
a little light somewhere makes a brighter
light everywhere. You can — and you
do — make a wonderful contribution to
this world.

— Douglas Pagels

Being True to Yourself
Is the Way God
Meant for You to Be

Being true to yourself
is the best way to go through life —
not trying to mimic others
but allowing your personality to shine.
Being who you are is the best way to be,
since God made you
and wanted you to follow the path
created in your honor.
He put your thoughts into place
as He did for no one else;
He gave you hopes and dreams
and desires uniquely yours.

God let your heart be the one
to envision something different.
He made your plans
for the future entirely your own.
So why not go along with His plan
and allow yourself
that beautiful privilege of living your life
as the one person who can do it best?

Be yourself…
because that is how you
were uniquely made
and wonderfully created.

— Barbara J. Hall

God Is at Work
in Your Life

You exist in a spiritual as well as a material universe. Life is large, mysterious, and miraculous. Remember that God is your source, and something greater than you is at work in your life.

Instead of limiting yourself to what you see or to past experience, open yourself to the infinite possibilities of what can be. Choose to believe that something larger than yourself is at work for you. That is the starting point for all the good things life has to offer. Trust this larger life to support and sustain you. Trust a wisdom greater than your limited knowledge to be provider and guide in all situations, for the highest good of all.

— Candy Paull

Only God knows your full potential, and He is guiding you toward that best version of yourself all the time. He has many tools and is never in a hurry. That can be frustrating for us, but even in our frustration, God is at work to produce patience in us. He never gets discouraged by how long it takes, and He delights every time you grow. Only God can see the "best version of you," and He is more concerned with you reaching your full potential than you are....

You are not *your* handiwork; your life is not your project. Your life is *God's* project. God thought you up, and He knows what you were intended to be.

— John Ortberg

You have been chosen to *transcend* —
to transcend the boundaries of your
own hopes and dreams, to transcend the
boundaries of your own plans and purposes,
and to transcend the borders of your own
family and friends. You have been chosen
to transcend the furthest reach of your own
definition of glory to be part of a greater glory,
the glory of God and His work of making all
things new.

— Paul David Tripp

Live Each Day
to the Fullest

Each day we can get up inspired by the reality that it is a new day. Yesterday is over — past. You have the opportunity to live today with a positive outlook. You can make the choice to be grateful, focusing on all you have rather than what you don't...

Live with zeal, relishing each minute ☆ Choose to see the beauty around you and revel in the glory of creation ☆ Experience joy and wonder through your senses ☆ See the world from a new perspective ☆ Look closely and be amazed at the awesomeness and intricacies of it all ☆ Embrace and be embraced ☆ Feel closeness and connection through a loving touch ☆ Speak kindly, encourage someone, and compliment others freely ☆ Say thank you from the heart and sing out loud just for the joy of it ☆ Have heart-to-heart talks, listen with openness to others, and take note so you remember what is important to them ☆

Let music lift you up ☆ Dance when you feel like it ☆ Enjoy all that life encompasses, pursue goals you only dreamed of before, and give in to your instincts to create ☆ Express love and affection ☆ Love yourself and others ☆ Give and receive freely ☆ Smile ☆ Let laughter be a natural response to the little pleasures in each moment ☆ Be filled with hope and expectation that this new day is full of potential ☆

— Janice Pettit

Do Your Best and Let God Take Care of the Rest

You have the strength it takes
and enough faith and courage too.
If you just take it step by step,
you can see anything through.

Blessings come in many ways.
All wrapped up in your dreams
are the hopes you have
and the prayers you pray.
You've just got to believe.

Each sunrise gives you a golden
chance to do your very best.
Just do all that you can
    day by day...

        and let God take care
            of the rest.

        — Alin Austin

I refuse to worry about anything.
I have complete confidence that the God
   who is always with me is able and
   willing to direct everything I do, to
   control my affairs, to lead me into
   the pathway of peace and happiness.
I free myself from every sense of
   condemnation, either against myself
   or others.
I lose every sense of animosity.
I now understand that there is a Principle
   and a Presence in every person gradually
   drawing him into the Kingdom of God.
I know that the Kingdom of God is at hand,
   and I am resolved to enter into this
   Kingdom, to possess it, and to let it
   possess me.
                              — Ernest Holmes

The answers we need
can be found inside our hearts —
where God has placed them
until we are ready to listen.
Let God guide you in all you do.
He will show you the road
you are meant to travel,
and He will walk beside you.

When you are frightened and weary
and it becomes hard to take
even one more step…
trust that He will carry you
and take your burdens.

— Jason Blume

☆ God is a well overflowing with living waters.

☆ He will quench your thirst for a rich and deeply spiritual life.

☆ He is a constant guardian looking over your shoulder.

☆ Whatever you know, God knows more.

You Are Part
of a Divine Plan

It may seem to many that the One who made us is too far removed to concern Himself with such tiny details of life on this old globe. But that is not the case. His mysterious plan is running its course right on schedule, exactly as He decreed it.

This world is not out of control, spinning wildly through space. Nor are earth's inhabitants at the mercy of some blind, random fate. When God created the world and set the stars in space, He also established the course of this world and His plan for humanity.

— Charles R. Swindoll

"For I know the plans I have for you," declares the Lord, "plans to prosper you and not to harm you, plans to give you hope and a future."

— Jeremiah 29:11(NIV)

How do you feel knowing that you are God's partner, knowing that you are part of God's divine plan? Can you see that you are not alone and that your efforts contribute to everyone else's? What can you do to further God's dream? What can you do in your family, in your community, in the world to create more caring, more sharing, more compassion, more laughter, and more peace?

— Desmond Tutu

You didn't come into this world
to live a mediocre life.
You came here purposefully,
fearlessly,
and joyfully.

When you feel inspired to rise
higher than you ever have before...
when you believe in your heart
that you can achieve your dreams...
when you know anything is possible
and you focus on that with all your being...
then you are connected
with the Creator within,
and all you truly want will come to you.
Follow your heart's desire.
Allow your Highest Self to lead you.
Live to embrace absolute joy
and complete abundance,
for this is indeed a life worth living
and one that will always
make you happy.
                                    — Lisa J. Butler

Know That God
Is with You Always

"I am always with you."
This is the promise of God to one and all —
to every heart that's hurting, grieving,
or burdened with pain.
He offers hope and comfort.
He offers caring and companionship.
He offers peace of mind.
God didn't say the sun would always shine
upon each day.
He didn't say the flowers would always bloom.
He didn't say time would always bring us
perfect happiness.
But God gave humanity a place to go —
a place where peace is always offered,
comfort is always given,
and love is a constant thing.
God said, "I am always with you,"
and He always is.

— Barbara J. Hall

☆ God is there when you feel tired, overwhelmed, or stressed. Inhale and exhale deeply, and feel His presence.

☆ God is there when you feel like nothing is going your way. Talk to Him, and He will show you the blessings you've been given.

☆ God is there when you feel desperate and alone. You only have to summon up the strength to ask for His help.

☆ God is there when you feel weak. Know that He will reach out His hand to you.

God is with you in the morning
He's with you in the night
He sees through every tear-stained glass
    window of your soul
He loves you just the way you are
    even when you feel you are nothing
He knows the question and the answer
    and the way to reach your goal

He's with you in the good times
    when everything is perfect
He's with you in the bad times
    when you have lost your way
He knows the fears that confront you
    and keep you from receiving
He sees the faith in all your efforts
    and hears every prayer you pray

He's in the thoughts that tiptoe barefoot
    along the banks of your heart
He's the landlord of your soul and
    your mind
He won't impose His will on you, but
    He'll help you make your own choices
    when you struggle for the answers that
    you want so much to find

He made the wonders of the universe
the sun and moon and stars
the rain clouds and the water in the
cool country stream
He's in your father and your mother
and every good-luck, four-leaf clover
He lives in your heart and knows every
dream you dream

When you think you're alone in this place
called life, don't be afraid
God is with you all the time
— Donna Fargo

It's Easy to Get in Touch with God...

☆ God never calls in sick.

☆ He never takes off two weeks for vacation.

☆ He doesn't require you to make an appointment.

☆ He won't put you on hold when you call.

☆ He makes time for you each and every day.

All It Takes Is a Simple Prayer

Prayer is a way that our hearts
   can communicate in faith,
a way that we can ask questions
   and receive answers,
a way that we can openly express
   our feelings and concerns.
Prayer is a wonderful source of
   strength for a person,
and prayers can become even
   stronger when we turn to each
   other for support in prayer.
Lean on prayer to help you through
   difficult times,
and know with certainty what the
   power of prayer can do.

— Susan Hickman Sater

Believe that God hears you when you pray and responds when you call on Him. That's what faith is... believing your prayer is answered.

Share with Him your feelings and remember that He said, "Be not afraid. I am with you and I will always be. Do not fret or have any anxiety about anything." Don't forget to praise Him and honor Him with your trust, your confidence, and your gratitude.

God has said He wants you to have
the desires of your heart, that He
loves you and wants you to have an
abundant life. Trust in the fact that
He's as good as His word. Rest in
the attitude that all things will work
for your good, and believe it.

— Donna Fargo

Dear God…

Help me to have the courage
to stand up for what I believe is right.
Protect me from those who are
unkind or hurtful.
Guide me to make sound decisions.
Help me temper my anger,
even when it is easier to lose control.
Remind me to appreciate all I have
and not mourn for what I have lost
or never had.

Keep me safe while I take time to heal.
Help me to keep an open mind
while I explore new options.
Never let me become bitter or give up
when I am overwhelmed with challenges.
Bless me with
the support of faithful friends.
Shine a ray of optimism into my life
to help me realize that this time will pass.
Thank you for watching over me.

Amen.

— Perri Elizabeth Hogan

God Loves Everything About You...

⭐ Your voice.

⭐ Your hair.

⭐ Your mind.

⭐ Your style.

⭐ Your smile.

⭐ Your heart.

God loves you. The eternal, self-existent Being who created and sustains everything that exists dearly loves you. The profound thought of God's love should begin and end your every day. It should define your every goal, your every action.

And He doesn't merely like you when you do well; He is personally and passionately committed to your good, even when you fail. God *loves* you.

— Dr. David Jeremiah

He Wants You to Remember…

You are a child of noble birth — a child of God ☆ You can do anything you put your mind to ☆ Learn to dream with your eyes wide open ☆ Pray as if it all depends on God; live as if it all depends on you ☆ Do as much as possible and trust God with the rest ☆ Love those who are most unlovable; they are His children too ☆ You were born to shine — let your inner light illuminate the world ☆ Forgive everyone everything, even when it's tough ☆ Be nice — you'll never regret being too kind ☆

Always be a hug waiting to happen ☆ If you want rainbows, you gotta have rain ☆ When life gives you a second chance, take it ☆ Stop what you're doing and start living ☆ Expect miracles ☆ Call home often ☆ Rise by lifting others ☆ Practice the art of listening ☆ And the most important thing God wants you to know is that, yes, it *is* a test and you're passing with flying colors! ☆

— Suzy Toronto

He Will See You Through the Hard Times

Sometimes in life, the path we desire may take us places we do not understand. But if we trust in God, He can lead us to the right path — the path to our destiny, the path that will fulfill our deepest desires and grant us peace of mind.

May the Lord grant you the vision to see your path. May He give you the discernment to know it is the right one. May He grant you the courage to walk down it and the strength to endure if you ever want to turn back. May God grant you the faith to always trust in Him on your journey.

Take courage and stand strong. Even though the future at times may seem uncertain, trust God to be your constant — your light to lead the way.

— Joanne Simon

Having a close relationship with God doesn't mean that you will never have problems, but it does mean that when you do, He will be there to help you. He will calm the storms in your life when things get rough. He will take the tough challenges you face and either transform them, enable you to rise above them, or help you walk through them successfully.

— Stormie Omartian

It takes a lot of effort to carry on when your body hurts or when you want to change an almost impossible situation. It takes strength and wisdom to believe in something you can't see.

It takes determination on your part to refuse to give up when the cards are stacked against you. After you've done all you know to do, it is time to trust in the Lord.

Sometimes you can get so down and out that hope will not come to your rescue and words land only on deaf ears. When this happens, you must fill up your cup with spiritual thoughts based on a higher authority than yourself.

Shine out every dark corner with the light of God's word. Meditate on certain scriptures and believe they are personally true to you. Speak your desires aloud as though they are already accomplished, with a sincere "thank you" attached. Plant positive seeds every way you turn. Allow yourself to dream and believe in the impossible. Don't let yourself be consumed by misery and discomfort. Don't believe anything that tries to make you think that things will never change. Let your attitude and behavior tell your body, mind, and spirit to honor you. Trust in the Lord and don't give up!

— Donna Fargo

God Has Put You on a Journey

God has a journey for *your* life. It looks different than anyone else's. The road He's carved out for you is yours alone. It's always the road less traveled because you're the only one who is ever going to walk it. Oh, sure, He'll give you wonderful traveling companions to go with you. But don't let that fool you: that doesn't mean their paths are the same as yours — just that they're parallel for a time....

Your GPS (God Positioning System) is going to get *you* exactly where you need to go. And He promises to be with you every step of the way.

— Holley Gerth

You're on the journey of a lifetime... a journey no one else will travel and no one else can judge — a path of happiness and hurt, where the challenges are great and the rewards even greater.

You're on a journey where each experience will teach you something valuable and you can't get lost, for you already know the way by heart.

You're on a journey that is universal yet uniquely personal, and profound yet astonishingly simple — where sometimes you will stumble and other times you will soar. You'll learn that even at your darkest point you can find a light — if you look for it. At the most difficult crossroad, you'll have an answer — if you listen for it. Friends and family will accompany you part of the way, and you'll walk the rest by yourself... but you will never be alone.

— Paula Finn

When You Feel like You Don't Measure Up, Remember These Truths...

☆ God doesn't judge you as harshly as you may judge yourself.

☆ He always gives you a second chance — no questions asked.

☆ He doesn't stop loving you because you made a mistake.

☆ He is always watching, but He doesn't keep score.

☆ You do not have to earn God's favor; you were born with it.

☆ You do not have to prove yourself worthy of God's love; He has already given it to you without condition.

☆ You do not have to beg God's forgiveness; it flows in your veins.

☆ You do not have to seek His attention; He is always listening.

☆ Nothing you do could ever drive God away.

You're in God's Heart Forever

In every storm, God's grace is watching over you. Even in the longest night, He is the promise of the dawn. No matter how long the journey, God is there. In these trying moments, may His love be all you feel.

God understands what you're going through... and He cares. Take courage from knowing God is by your side. When life gets complicated and things seem overwhelming, God is a rainbow over you. No matter what a day may bring, God is greater than any challenge. He knows what you are dealing with; He sees every sigh and tear. Just be strong in knowing God is near.

There are times when all we can do is wait — and the only gift we can give is prayer. Remember God's promise of better days ahead, brighter skies, and happier times. His heart is full of hope for you. He's by your side from dawn to dusk; rest safely in His care. May you find peace in every promise His heart holds for you. May thoughts of love whisper to you... "God who holds the stars in place... always holds you in His heart."

— Linda E. Knight

Acknowledgments

We gratefully acknowledge the permission granted by the following authors and authors' representatives to reprint poems or excerpts from their publications: Lisa Mae Huddleston for "God Loves You Just the Way You Are" and "Trust in God's Dream for Your Life." Copyright © 2014 by Lisa Mae Huddleston. All rights reserved. Amanda Rowe for "The Meaning of Faith." Copyright © 2014 by Amanda Rowe. All rights reserved. Rachel Snyder for "When all else fades and melts away...." Copyright © 2014 by Rachel Snyder. All rights reserved. Dzana Madagu for "Believe in How Special You Are." Copyright © 2014 by Dzana Madagu. All rights reserved. Jeff Seaman for "When God made you..." from "Why God Made You" (SermonCentral.com: April 26, 2001). Copyright © 2001 by Jeff Seaman. All rights reserved. WaterBrook Multnomah, an imprint of the Crown Publishing Group, a division of Random House, Inc., for "There has never been and never will be..." from SOUL PRINT: DISCOVERING YOUR DIVINE DESTINY by Mark Batterson. Copyright © 2001 by Mark Batterson. All rights reserved. Any third party use of this material, outside of this publication, is prohibited. PrimaDonna Entertainment Corp. for "God Gifted You to Do Something Special," "God is with you in the morning...," "Believe that God hears you...," and "It takes a lot of effort..." by Donna Fargo. Copyright © 2014 by PrimaDonna Entertainment Corp. All rights reserved. Jason Blume for "You Are God's Masterpiece," "May God Grant You These Gifts," and "The answers we need...." Copyright © 2006, 2013, 2014 by Jason Blume. All rights reserved. Thomas Nelson, Inc., Nashville, Tennessee, for "When God sees you..." by Jenna Lucado Bishop from YOU WERE MADE TO MAKE A DIFFERENCE by Max Lucado and Jenna Lucado Bishop. Copyright © 2010 by Max Lucado. All rights reserved. And for "It may seem to many..." from THE MYSTERY OF GOD'S WILL by Charles R. Swindoll. Copyright © 1999 by Charles R. Swindoll, Inc. All rights reserved. Caroline J. Hewitt for "True strength is measured...." Copyright © 2014 by Caroline J. Hewitt. All rights reserved. Perri Elizabeth Hogan for "Hold on to Your Faith" and "Dear God...." Copyright © 2014 by Perri Elizabeth Hogan. All rights reserved. Candy Paull for "Angels Are Watching over You" and "God Is at Work in Your Life." Copyright © 2014 by Candy Paull. All rights reserved. Debbie Burton-Peddle for "God Doesn't Expect Perfection." Copyright © 2014 by Debbie Burton-Peddle. All rights reserved. Lamisha Serf for "We Are All Works in Progress." Copyright © 2014 by Lamisha Serf. All rights reserved. Barbara J. Hall for "A Prayer for Help" and "Being True to Yourself Is the Way God Meant for You to Be." Copyright © 2014 by Barbara J. Hall. All rights reserved. Cathleen Zeller for "Wouldn't every day be wonderful...." Copyright © 2014 by Cathleen Zeller. All rights reserved. Zondervan, www.zondervan.com, for "Only God knows your full potential..." from THE ME I WANT TO BE: BECOMING GOD'S BEST VERSION OF YOU by John Ortberg. Copyright © 2010 by John Ortberg. All rights reserved. New Growth Press for "You have been chosen to transcend..." from A QUEST FOR MORE: LIVING FOR SOMETHING BIGGER THAN YOU by Paul David Tripp. Copyright © 2007, 2008 by Paul David Tripp. All rights reserved. Janice Pettit for "Live Each Day to the Fullest." Copyright © 2014 by Janice Pettit. All rights reserved. Founders Church of Religious Science for "I refuse to worry about anything" from THIS THING CALLED YOU by Ernest Holmes. Copyright © 1948 by Ernest Holmes. All rights reserved. Doubleday, a division of Random House, Inc., for "How do you feel knowing that..." from GOD HAS A DREAM: A VISION OF HOPE FOR OUR TIME by Desmond Tutu. Copyright © 2004 by Desmond Tutu. All rights reserved. Lisa J. Butler for "You didn't come into this world...." Copyright © 2014 by Lisa J. Butler. All rights reserved. Susan Hickman Sater for "All It Takes Is a Simple Prayer." Copyright © 2014 by Susan Hickman Sater. All rights reserved. FaithWords, a division of Hachette Book Group, for "God loves you" from GOD LOVES YOU: HE ALWAYS HAS — HE ALWAYS WILL by Dr. David Jeremiah. Copyright © 2012 by David Jeremiah. All rights reserved. Reprinted by permission. Suzy Toronto for "He Wants You to Remember...." Copyright © 2012 by Suzy Toronto. All rights reserved. Joanne Simon for "Sometimes in life...." Copyright © 2014 by Joanne Simon. All rights reserved. Harvest House Publishers, www.harvesthousepublishers.com, for "Having a close relationship with God..." from THE POWER OF A PRAYING® TEEN by Stormie Omartian. Copyright © 2005 by Stormie Omartian. All rights reserved. Used by permission. Revell, a division of Baker Publishing Group, for "God has a journey for your life" from YOU'RE ALREADY AMAZING by Holley Gerth. Copyright © 2002 by Holley Gerth. All rights reserved. Paula Finn for "You're on the journey of a lifetime...." Copyright © 2013 by Paula Finn. All rights reserved. Linda E. Knight for "You're in God's Heart Forever." Copyright © 2014 by Linda E. Knight. All rights reserved.

A careful effort has been made to trace the ownership of selections used in this anthology in order to obtain permission to reprint copyrighted material and give proper credit to the copyright owners. If any error or omission has occurred, it is completely inadvertent, and we would like to make corrections in future editions provided that written notification is made to the publisher:

BLUE MOUNTAIN ARTS, INC., P.O. Box 4549, Boulder, Colorado 80306.